WHALES SET I

KILLER WHALES

Megan M. Gunderson
ABDO Publishing Company

visit us at
www.abdopublishing.com

Published by ABDO Publishing Company, 8000 West 78th Street, Edina, Minnesota 55439.
Copyright © 2011 by Abdo Consulting Group, Inc. International copyrights reserved in all
countries. No part of this book may be reproduced in any form without written permission
from the publisher. The Checkerboard Library™ is a trademark and logo of ABDO
Publishing Company.

Printed in the United States of America, North Mankato, Minnesota.
042010
092010

 PRINTED ON RECYCLED PAPER

Cover Photo: Photolibrary
Interior Photos: © Hiroya Minakuchi / SeaPics.com p. 13; iStockphoto pp. 8, 11, 14;
    © Michael S. Nolan / SeaPics.com p. 17; Peter Arnold pp. 5, 15, 21; Photolibrary p. 18;
    Uko Gorter pp. 7, 9

Editor: BreAnn Rumsch
Art Direction & Cover Design: Neil Klinepier

Library of Congress Cataloging-in-Publication Data

Gunderson, Megan M., 1981-
  Killer whales / Megan M. Gunderson.
      p. cm. -- (Whales)
  Includes index.
  ISBN 978-1-61613-450-1
  1. Killer whale--Juvenile literature. I. Title.
  QL737.C432.G8594 2010
  599.53'6--dc22
                                              2010006442

CONTENTS

KILLER WHALES AND FAMILY

Killer whales were once feared by sea creatures and humans alike! Sailors called them whale killers, which inspired their name. Killer whales do attack other **cetaceans**. But, they are not known to have killed any humans in the wild.

These curious creatures are mammals. That means killer whales are **warm-blooded** and nurse their young. To breathe, they open a single blowhole on the head. They fill their lungs with air at the water's surface.

Killer whales belong to the family Delphinidae. This family contains about 36 species, including bottlenose dolphins and pilot whales. Killer whales are the largest members of their family.

The killer whale's large brain weighs around 12 pounds (6 kg).

SHAPE, SIZE, AND COLOR

Most people easily recognize the killer whale. It has a large body, a **blunt** beak, and huge, rounded flippers. A male's flippers can reach 7 feet (2 m) long. Males also have tall, straight dorsal fins. These can grow 6 feet (1.8 m) high! Females and young killer whales have smaller dorsal fins that curve backward.

Male killer whales often grow more than 26 feet (8 m) long. They weigh around 10,000 pounds (4,500 kg). Females only reach about 23 feet (7 m) in length. They weigh much less than males.

Smooth black skin with white markings makes killer whales stand out. They are white on their bellies and the undersides of their flukes. White

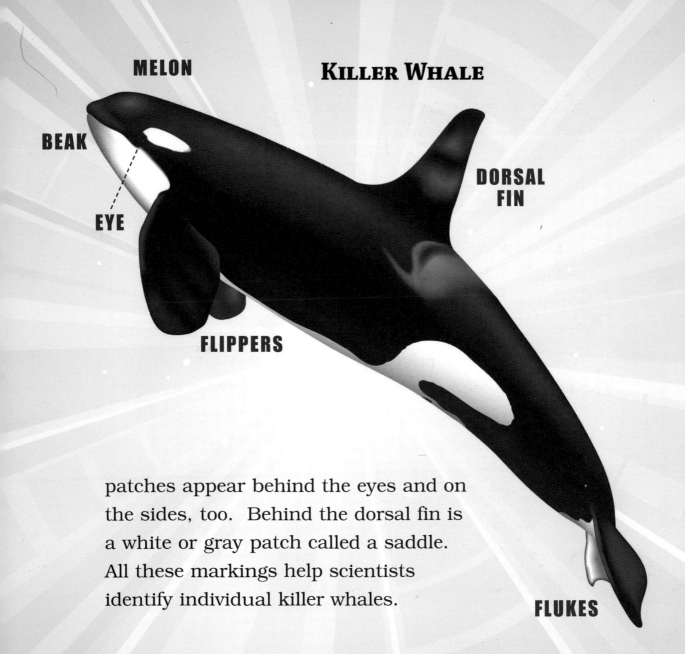

MELON

KILLER WHALE

BEAK

EYE

DORSAL FIN

FLIPPERS

FLUKES

patches appear behind the eyes and on the sides, too. Behind the dorsal fin is a white or gray patch called a saddle. All these markings help scientists identify individual killer whales.

WHERE THEY LIVE

Killer whales may have the largest range of any mammal except humans. They live in oceans around the world.

Killer whales are more common in cool waters than in warm waters.

Usually, killer whales stay within 500 miles (800 km) of a coast. They even enter river mouths, **estuaries**, and bays.

Where Do Killer Whales Live?

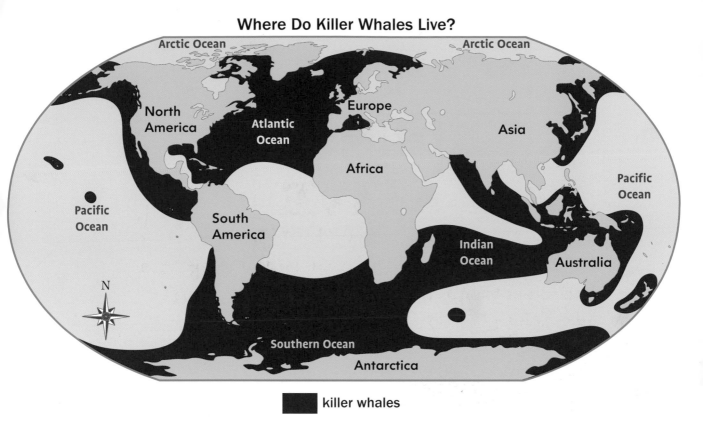

killer whales

Unlike many **cetaceans**, killer whales travel easily from one **hemisphere** to another. They go where the food is. Killer whales can **migrate** long distances. For example, some travel between Alaska and California. Others stay in one area year-round.

Senses

Killer whales are constantly looking and listening as they swim through their **habitats**. Their eyesight works well in and above water. So, killer whales spyhop. They bob their heads up out of the water to check out their surroundings!

A good sense of hearing is an important part of echolocation. To use echolocation, a killer whale sends a series of clicks out through its **melon**. These hit objects in the animal's path and bounce back as echoes. The killer whale listens for these echoes. They tell it an object's size, speed, and distance.

Killer whales appear to have a well-developed sense of touch. Scientists believe the skin is most sensitive around the mouth, blowhole, and eyes.

Spyhopping is a common behavior in many whale species.

Scientists do not believe killer whales can smell.
But, these whales do have taste buds. They seem
to prefer the taste of some foods over others.

DEFENSE

Sharks may attack injured, young, or old killer whales. Healthy, adult killer whales have no known natural predators. Humans are their main enemies.

Killer whales are fast swimmers. They can reach 28 miles per hour (45 km/h). So, they may be able to swim away from some dangers. However, most human threats are difficult to avoid.

Pollution affects the health of killer whales and their **habitats**. Boats injure killer whales, too. And, the noises boats make can affect the ability to use echolocation. Killer whales also become tangled in fishing gear.

Another threat to killer whales is overfishing. With less fish available, killer whales may not find enough to eat. Fewer fish also means less food for other marine mammals. This may decrease populations of larger animals that killer whales also depend on for food.

Pollution of ocean waters threatens killer whale populations.

FOOD

Killer whales are carnivores! They will feast on salmon, tuna, herring, squid, and rays. Sea turtles, penguins, and sharks are other tasty treats. Different groups of killer whales often focus on specific prey.

Killer whales are most known for eating other mammals. They devour otters, seals, sea lions, and whales of all sizes. They even catch deer and moose that go out for a swim!

To herd fish, killer whales work together. They also cooperate to hunt large whales. To get at onshore prey, killer whales will **beach**

A killer whale's strong jaws hold up to 56 teeth. Each tooth is about 4 inches (10 cm) long!

Killer whales will grab sea lions from the water's edge!

themselves. They even ram ice from below to knock penguins into the water.

Killer whales catch prey in their large, cone-shaped teeth. The teeth curve inward and interlock to hold prey tight. Killer whales rip larger prey into pieces they can easily swallow.

BABIES

Killer whales mate at any time of year. Afterward, a female may become **pregnant**. She carries her baby for 15 to 18 months. The baby is called a calf.

Newborn killer whales weigh 350 to 450 pounds (160 to 200 kg). They are already 7 to 8.5 feet (2.1 to 2.6 m) long at birth!

Calves depend on their mothers for safety and food. The calves learn to eat solid food very early. But, they still nurse for one to two years.

Killer whales may stay with their mothers even after they become adults. Male killer whales live for up to 60 years. Females can live until they are 90 years old!

On average, a female killer whale gives birth to five calves during her lifetime. She stops having babies around age 40.

BEHAVIORS

Killer whales are very social animals that live in **pods**. These groups vary from just a few individuals to around 50 members. Herds of more than 500 killer whales form when many pods join together.

Pods are usually a mix of males, females, and young. Pod members care for one another. They even help those that are injured or ill.

To communicate with each other, killer whales make a variety of sounds. Each group has a **unique** set of calls. These help group members recognize each other and stay organized. Killer whales in different parts of the world have different dialects.

Killer whales may also communicate with actions above water. They slap their flukes, dorsal fins, and flippers on the water's surface. Scientists think these actions may help killer whales scratch itches, too! There is much left to discover about the lives of killer whales.

Killer whales often breach. They leap out of the water and land with a splash!

KILLER WHALE FACTS

Scientific Name: *Orcinus orca*

Common Name: Killer whale

Other Names: Orca

Average Size:
Length - 23 to 26 feet (7 to 8 m)
Weight - 10,000 pounds (4,500 kg) for males, but females weigh much less

Where They Are Found: In all oceans, especially near coasts

Many people call killer whales orcas.

GLOSSARY

beach - to strand on a beach.

blunt - rounded.

cetacean (sih-TAY-shuhn) - a member of the order Cetacea. Mammals such as dolphins, whales, and porpoises are cetaceans.

estuary (EHS-chuh-wehr-ee) - the area of water where a river's current meets an ocean's tide.

habitat - a place where a living thing is naturally found.

hemisphere - one half of Earth.

melon - a rounded structure found in the forehead of some cetaceans.

migrate - to move from one place to another, often to find food.

pod - a group of socially connected dolphins or whales.

pregnant - having one or more babies growing within the body.

unique - being thc only one of its kind.

warm-blooded - having a body temperature that is not much affected by surrounding air or water.

WEB SITES

To learn more about killer whales, visit ABDO Publishing Company on the World Wide Web at **www.abdopublishing.com**. Web sites about killer whales are featured on our Book Links page. These links are routinely monitored and updated to provide the most current information available.

INDEX